I0500611

December 2012

BORDER SECURITY

Additional Actions Needed to Strengthen CBP Efforts to Mitigate Risk of Employee Corruption and Misconduct

G A O
Accountability ★ Integrity ★ Reliability

GAO-13-59

Highlights

Highlights of GAO-13-59, a report to congressional requesters

BORDER SECURITY

Additional Actions Needed to Strengthen CBP Efforts to Mitigate Risk of Employee Corruption and Misconduct

Why GAO Did This Study

CBP—a component within the Department of Homeland Security— is responsible for securing U.S. borders and facilitating legal travel and trade. Drug-trafficking and other transnational criminal organizations are seeking to target CBP employees with bribes to facilitate the illicit transport of drugs, aliens, and other contraband across the southwest U.S. border, in particular. CBP IA is responsible for promoting the integrity of CBP's workforce, programs, and operations; and CBP components implement integrity initiatives. GAO was asked to review CBP's efforts to ensure the integrity of its workforce. This report examines (1) data on arrests of and allegations against CBP employees for corruption or misconduct, (2) CBP's implementation of integrity-related controls, and (3) CBP's strategy for its integrity programs. GAO analyzed arrest and allegation data since fiscal year 2005 and 2006, respectively, reviewed integrity-related policies and procedures, and interviewed CBP officials in headquarters and at four locations along the southwest border selected for geographic location, among other factors.

What GAO Recommends

GAO recommends that CBP, among other things, track and maintain data on sources of information used to determine which applicants are unsuitable for hire, assess the feasibility of expanding the polygraph program to incumbent officers and agents, consistently conduct quality assurance reviews, and set timelines for completing and implementing a comprehensive integrity strategy. DHS concurred and reported taking steps to address the recommendations.

View GAO-13-59. For more information, contact Rebecca Gambler at (202) 512-8777 or gamblerr@gao.gov.

What GAO Found

U.S. Customs and Border Protection (CBP) data indicate that arrests of CBP employees for corruption-related activities since fiscal years 2005 account for less than 1 percent of CBP's entire workforce per fiscal year. The majority of arrests of CBP employees were related to misconduct. There were 2,170 reported incidents of arrests for acts of misconduct such as domestic violence or driving under the influence from fiscal year 2005 through fiscal year 2012, and a total of 144 current or former CBP employees were arrested or indicted for corruption-related activities, such as the smuggling of aliens and drugs, of whom 125 have been convicted as of October 2012. Further, the majority of allegations against CBP employees since fiscal year 2006 occurred at locations along the southwest border. CBP officials have stated that they are concerned about the negative impact that these cases have on agencywide integrity.

CBP employs screening tools to mitigate the risk of employee corruption and misconduct for both applicants (e.g., background investigations and polygraph examinations) and incumbent CBP officers and Border Patrol agents (e.g., random drug tests and periodic reinvestigations). However, CBP's Office of Internal Affairs (IA) does not have a mechanism to maintain and track data on which of its screening tools (e.g., background investigation or polygraph examination) provided the information used to determine which applicants were not suitable for hire. Maintaining and tracking such data is consistent with internal control standards and could better position CBP IA to gauge the relative effectiveness of its screening tools. CBP IA is also considering requiring periodic polygraphs for incumbent officers and agents; however, it has not yet fully assessed the feasibility of expanding the program. For example, CBP has not yet fully assessed the costs of implementing polygraph examinations on incumbent officers and agents, including costs for additional supervisors and adjudicators, or factors such as the trade-offs associated with testing incumbent officers and agents at various frequencies. A feasibility assessment of program expansion could better position CBP to determine whether and how to best achieve its goal of strengthening integrity-related controls for officers and agents. Further, CBP IA has not consistently conducted monthly quality assurance reviews of its adjudications since 2008, as required by internal policies, to help ensure that adjudicators are following procedures in evaluating the results of the preemployment and periodic background investigations. CBP IA officials stated that they have performed some of the required checks since 2008, but they could not provide data on how many checks were conducted. Without these quality assurance checks, it is difficult for CBP IA to determine the extent to which deficiencies, if any, exist in the adjudication process.

CBP does not have an integrity strategy, as called for in its *Fiscal Year 2009-2014 Strategic Plan*. During the course of our review, CBP IA began drafting a strategy, but CBP IA's Assistant Commissioner stated the agency has not set target timelines for completing and implementing this strategy. Moreover, he stated that there has been significant cultural resistance among some CBP components in acknowledging CBP IA's authority for overseeing all integrity-related activities. Setting target timelines is consistent with program management standards and could help CBP monitor progress made toward the development and implementation of an agencywide strategy.

_____ United States Government Accountability Office

Contents

Abbreviations

AMSCO	Analytical Management Systems and Control Office
BI	background investigation
BPA	U.S. Border Patrol agent
CAD	Credibility Assessment Division
CBP	U.S. Customs and Border Protection
CBPO	U.S. Customs and Border Protection officer
DHS	Department of Homeland Security
IA	Office of Internal Affairs
IPCC	Integrity Integrated Planning and Coordination Committee
ISMS	Integrated Security Management System
JIC	Joint Intake Center
OFO	Office of Field Operations
OPM	Office of Personnel Management
PSD	Personnel Security Division
SSBI	single scope background investigation
USBP	U.S. Border Patrol

United States Government Accountability Office
Washington, DC 20548

December 4, 2012

The Honorable Tom Coburn
Ranking Member, Permanent Subcommittee on Investigations
Committee on Homeland Security and Governmental Affairs
United States Senate

The Honorable Michael T. McCaul
Chairman
Subcommittee on Oversight, Investigations, and Management
Committee on Homeland Security
House of Representatives

Drug-trafficking and other transnational criminal organizations have increasingly sought to target U.S. law enforcement personnel with bribes and other inducements to facilitate their illicit transport of drugs, aliens, and other contraband across the U.S. southwest border.[1] U.S. Customs and Border Protection (CBP), within the Department of Homeland Security (DHS), is responsible for securing U.S. borders and facilitating legal travel and trade. Specifically, officers from CBP's Office of Field Operations (OFO)[2] are responsible for securing the border at U.S. ports of entry, while CBP's U.S. Border Patrol agents (BPA) are responsible for securing the national border between the ports of entry.[3] CBP's Office of Internal Affairs (IA) is responsible for promoting the integrity of CBP's workforce, programs, and operations. For the purposes of our report, integrity issues include acts of corruption such as accepting cash bribes and other gratuities in return for allowing contraband or inadmissible

---

[1]The southwest U.S. border includes areas within the states of Arizona, California, New Mexico, and Texas.

[2]OFO, which is headed by an Assistant Commissioner, oversees nearly 28,000 employees who are responsible for providing security at U.S. ports of entry. A port of entry is a location by which individuals and merchandise may seek legal entry into the United States. There are 329 air, sea, and land ports in the United States; there are 25 land ports, in particular, along the southwest border.

[3]Officers and agents are responsible for apprehending individuals attempting to enter the United States illegally and stemming the flow of illegal drugs and other illicit contraband across the border, among other things.

aliens into the country, as well as other criminal activities or misconduct such as drug or alcohol abuse.[4]

DHS officials have testified that CBP's increased hiring of officers and agents since fiscal year 2006 has amplified the incentives and opportunities for attempted corruption of the CBP workforce through bribery, infiltration, or other means.[5] From fiscal years 2006 through 2011, the number of CBP officers (CBPOs) and BPAs along the southwest border increased from 15,792 to 24,057. Moreover, DHS officials have stated that drug-trafficking organizations are attempting to infiltrate the CBP workforce through conspired hiring operations and aggressive targeting of incumbent CBPOs and BPAs. In fiscal year 2012, CBP allocated approximately $166 million for integrity programs.

You asked us to review CBP's efforts to ensure the integrity of its workforce, and particularly for CBPOs and BPAs stationed along the southwest U.S. border. This report examines (1) data on arrests of and allegations against CBP employees accused of corruption or misconduct-related activities, (2) CBP's implementation of integrity-related controls to prevent and detect employee corruption and misconduct, and (3) CBP's strategy for implementing its integrity programs.

To examine data on arrests of and allegations against CBP employees accused of corruption or misconduct issues, we analyzed data on 144 CBP employees arrested or indicted from fiscal years 2005 through fiscal year 2012 for alleged corruption activities. We also analyzed data on

---

[4]We developed this definition on the basis of an analysis of data and documentation from CBP IA, as well as through interviews with CBP IA and law enforcement officials who investigate allegations of employee misconduct and corruption. We also discussed our definition with these officials to ensure that it was a reasonable interpretation and consistent with CBP policy.

[5]See Statement of Alan Bersin, Commissioner, U.S. Customs and Border Protection, before the Ad Hoc Subcommittee on Disaster Recovery and Intergovernmental Affairs, Senate Committee on Homeland Security and Governmental Affairs. Washington, D.C.: June 9, 2011, and Statement of Charles K. Edwards, Acting Inspector General, Department of Homeland Security, before the Subcommittee on Government Organization, Efficiency, and Financial Management, Committee on Oversight and Government Report, House of Representatives. Washington, D.C.: Aug. 1, 2012. Statement of James F. Tomsheck, Assistant Commissioner, Office of Internal Affairs, U.S. Customs and Border Protection, before the Ad Hoc Subcommittee on State, Local and Sector Preparedness and Integration, Committee on Homeland Security and Governmental Affairs, Senate. Washington, D.C.:Mar. 11, 2010.

allegations of corruption and misconduct made against CBP employees from fiscal years 2006 through 2011.[6] For both arrest and allegation data, these are the time periods for which the most complete and reliable data were available. In particular, we analyzed variations in both sets of data across CBP components and geographic regions. To assess the reliability of these data, we (1) performed electronic data testing and looked for obvious errors in accuracy and completeness, and (2) interviewed agency officials knowledgeable about these data to determine the processes in place to ensure their accuracy. In addition, we interviewed CBP officials to gain their perspectives on these data. We determined that the data were sufficiently reliable for the purposes of this report.

To evaluate CBP's implementation of integrity-related controls to prevent and detect employee misconduct and corruption, we analyzed relevant laws such as the Anti-Border Corruption Act of 2010, which requires, by January 2013, that all CBPO and BPA applicants receive polygraph examinations before they are hired.[7] We also reviewed documentation on CBP's preemployment screening practices and their results—including background investigations and polygraph examinations—and relevant data and documentation on the random drug testing program and the periodic reinvestigation process for incumbent officers and agents. In particular, we evaluated CBP IA data on the technical results of polygraph examinations from January 2008 through August 2012.[8] To assess the reliability of these data, we (1) performed electronic data testing and looked for obvious errors in accuracy and completeness and (2) interviewed agency officials knowledgeable about these data to determine the processes in place to ensure their accuracy. We determined that these data were sufficiently reliable for the purposes of this report. In addition, we examined CBP IA's quality assurance program for its

---

[6]These data on allegations include what is available through CBP's Joint Intake Center (JIC), which is a central clearinghouse for allegations of misconduct involving personnel and contractors employed by CBP. Allegations reported to the DHS Office of Inspector General, the Federal Bureau of Investigation, or other law enforcement agencies may not be represented in JIC's data. According to CBP IA officials, if they become aware of an allegation against a CBP employee from another source, they create a record in JIC for tracking purposes.

[7]Pub. L. No. 111-376, § 3, 124 Stat. 4104, 4104-05 (2011).

[8]CBP began conducting polygraph examinations for some CBP employees in January 2008.

Personnel Security Division (PSD),[9] including interviewing PSD officials who are responsible for deciding whether an applicant or incumbent officer or agent is suitable for hire or continued employment.[10] We compared CBP's integrity-related controls, as applicable, with standards in *Standards for Internal Control in the Federal Government*[11] and standard practices from the Project Management Institute.[12] Furthermore, we conducted visits to four locations along the southwest U.S. border to observe the implementation of various integrity-related controls and obtain perspectives from CBP officials at these locations on the implementation of integrity-related controls.[13] We selected these locations on the basis of a variety of factors, including the colocation of CBP IA with OFO offices and U.S. Border Patrol (USBP) sectors along the southwest border and the number of allegations against or arrests of CBP employees for corruption or misconduct.[14] Because we selected a nonprobability sample of locations to visit, the information we obtained from these visits cannot be generalized to all field locations. However, observations obtained from these visits provided us with a greater understanding of CBP's integrity-related initiatives.

To evaluate CBP's integrity strategy, including how the agency incorporates lessons learned from prior misconduct and corruption cases, we reviewed CBP strategic planning documents and other policy

---

[9]PSD, within CBP IA, manages the personnel security and suitability program by initiating and adjudicating preemployment investigations for CBP applicants and contractors. PSD also conducts and adjudicates periodic reinvestigations and issues security clearances for CBP employees.

[10]With a favorable suitability determination, an applicant can be hired, if all other requirements are met. The suitability determination is a process that subjects applicants' and employees' personal conduct to evaluation throughout their careers. Title 5, Code of Federal Regulations Part 731, establishes factors that are used to make a determination of suitability.

[11]GAO, *Standards for Internal Control in the Federal Government*, GAO/AIMD-00-21.3.1 (Washington, D.C.: November 1999).

[12]Project Management Institute, *The Standard for Program Management*, second edition © (Newton Square, Pa., 2006, updated 2008).

[13]We conducted site visits in El Paso, Texas; Laredo, Texas; San Diego, California; and, Tucson, Arizona.

[14]Border Patrol sectors are further divided into stations, and each station is responsible for operations within a specific area of the sector. There are nine sectors along the southwest border.

statements on integrity initiatives. In particular, we analyzed these documents against the requirements set forth in CBP's *Fiscal Year 2009-2014 Strategic Plan*.[15] In addition, we analyzed all available postcorruption analyses reports, which identify deficiencies that may have enabled CBP employees to engage in corruption-related activities, against OFO and USBP program requirements. We interviewed CBP officials in Washington, D.C., as well as during our site visits, regarding CBP's integrity strategy and the extent to which CBP is using lessons learned from prior corruption and misconduct cases to guide changes in policies and procedures, as appropriate.

We conducted this performance audit from December 2011 to December 2012, in accordance with generally accepted government auditing standards. Those standards require that we plan and perform the audit to obtain sufficient, appropriate evidence to provide a reasonable basis for our findings and conclusions based on our audit objectives. We believe that the evidence obtained provides a reasonable basis for our findings and conclusions based on our audit objectives. Appendix I presents more details about our scope and methodology.

Background

CBP is the largest uniformed law enforcement agency in the United States, with approximately 21,400 BPAs patrolling between the nation's ports of entry and more than 20,000 CBPOs stationed at air, land, and seaports nationwide at the end of fiscal year 2011.[16] On the U.S. southwest border, there are about 5,500 CBPOs and 18,000 BPAs as of the end of fiscal year 2011. CBPOs, based within OFO, are responsible for processing immigration documentation of passengers and pedestrians and inspecting vehicles and cargo at U.S. ports of entry. BPAs are based within the USBP and are responsible for enforcing immigration laws across the territory in between the ports of entry and at checkpoints located inside the U.S. border. Together, CBPOs and BPAs are

---

[15]U.S.Customs and Border Protection. *Secure Borders, Safe Travel, Legal Trade: U.S. Customs and Border Protection Fiscal Year 2009-2014 Strategic Plan*. Washington, D.C.: July 2009.

[16]In fiscal years 2011 and 2012, appropriations acts provided that Border Patrol was to maintain an active duty presence of not less than 21,370 agents protecting the border of the United States. Department of Defense and Full-Year Continuing Appropriations Act, 2011, div. B, tit. VI, § 1608, Pub. L. No. 112-10, 125 Stat. 38, 140; Consolidated Appropriations Act, 2012, div. D, tit. II, Pub. L. No. 112-74, 125 Stat. 786, 945-46 (2011).

responsible for detecting and preventing the illegal entry of persons and contraband, including terrorists and weapons of mass destruction, across the border.

Hiring Process for CBPOs and BPAs

U.S. citizens interested in becoming CBPOs or BPAs must successfully complete all steps of the CBP hiring process, which includes an online application, a cognitive exam, fingerprint collection, financial disclosure, a structured interview, fitness tests, medical examinations, a polygraph examination, a background investigation, and a drug test. CBP IA's PSD manages the personnel security program by initiating and adjudicating preemployment investigations for CBP applicants, which aim to ensure that the candidates are reliable, trustworthy, and loyal to the United States, and therefore suitable for employment. In addition, CBP IA's Credibility Assessment Division (CAD) is responsible for administering the polygraph examinations, interviewing applicants, and collecting any admissions that an applicant may reveal including past criminal behavior or misconduct. Human Resource Management is responsible for making the hiring decisions based on the final suitability determination from CBP IA (this includes PSD's overall assessment of the polygraph examination and background investigation), as well as the applicant's successful completion of the other steps in the hiring process.

The number of CBP employees increased from 43,545 in fiscal year 2006 to 60,591 as of August 2012. During this time period, both OFO and USBP experienced a hiring surge and received increased appropriations to fund additional hiring of CBPOs and BPAs.[17] The majority of the newly hired CBPOs and BPAs were assigned to the southwest border. In particular, during this time period, their total numbers along the southwest border increased from 15,792 to 24,057. As of fiscal year 2011, 57

---

[17]For example, CBP received funds to support 1,000 additional Border Patrol agents in fiscal year 2006, 1,500 in fiscal year 2007, 3,000 in fiscal year 2008, and 1,100 in fiscal year 2010, among other increases. CBP also received funds for an additional 450 CBP officers in fiscal year 2007, 200 in fiscal year 2008, and 859 in fiscal year 2009, among other increases. See H.R. Rep. No. 109-241, at 41-42 (2005) (Conf. Rep.); H.R. Rep. No. 106-699, at 125, 128 (2006) (Conf. Rep.); Explanatory Statement, Consolidated Appropriations Act, 2008, bk. 1, div. E., at 1028 (2008); Explanatory Statement, Consolidated Security, Disaster Assistance, and Continuing Appropriations Act, 2009, div. D, at 627 (2008); H.R. Rep. No. 111-151, at 110 (2009) (Conf. Rep.); H.R. Rep. No. 111-298, at 62-63 (2009) (Conf. Rep.); Pub. L. No. 111-230, tit. I, 124 Stat. 2485, 2485 (2010); H.R. Rep. No. 112-331, at 956-57 (2011) (Conf. Rep.).

percent of the CBPOs and BPA were stationed along the southwest border. Figure 1 provides additional details.

Figure 1: CBPO and BPA Workforce Population Data, Fiscal Years 2006-2011

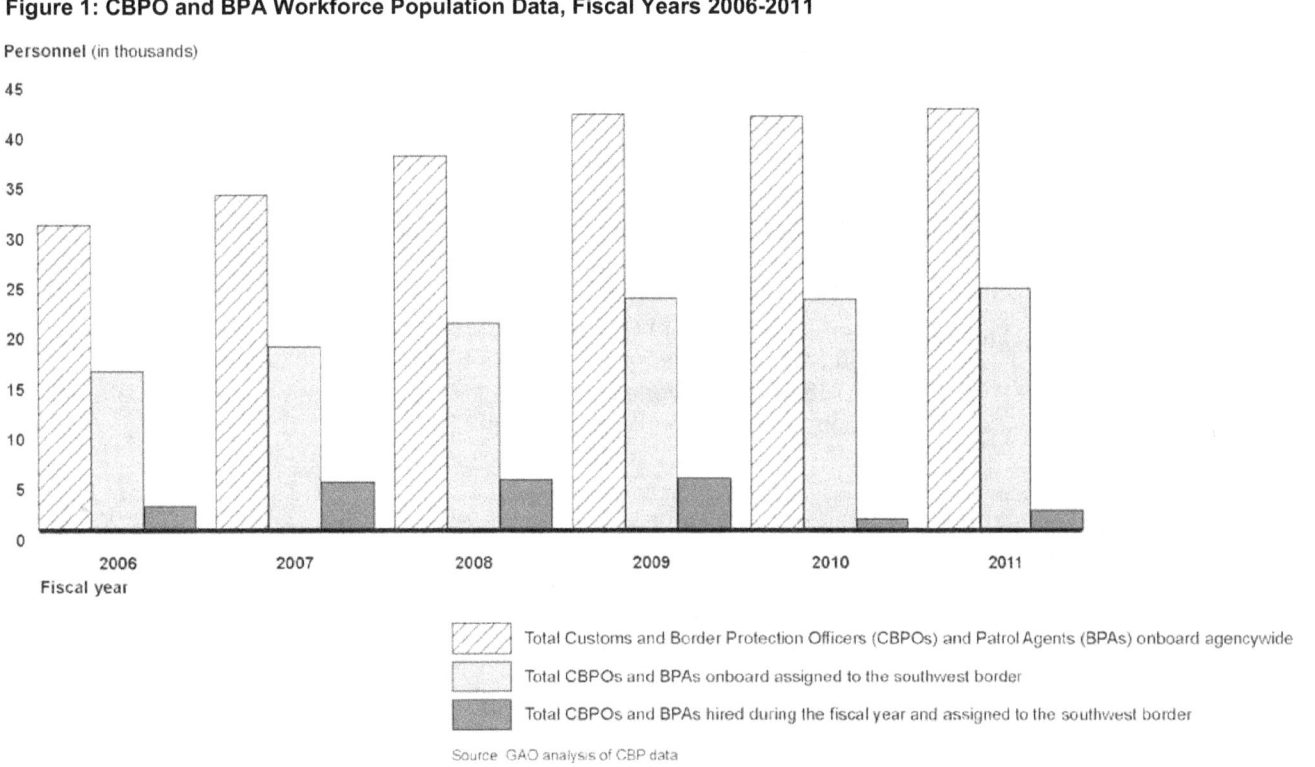

Source: GAO analysis of CBP data

Legend:
- Total Customs and Border Protection Officers (CBPOs) and Patrol Agents (BPAs) onboard agencywide
- Total CBPOs and BPAs onboard assigned to the southwest border
- Total CBPOs and BPAs hired during the fiscal year and assigned to the southwest border

Process for Reporting Allegations against CBP Employees

Allegations against CBP employees for misconduct, corruption, or other issues can be reported through various mechanisms. CBP IA, in partnership with the Office of Professional Responsibility—an office within DHS's U.S. Immigration and Customs Enforcement—accepts allegations through the Joint Intake Center (JIC). JIC is CBP's central clearinghouse for receiving, processing, and tracking all allegations of misconduct involving personnel and contractors employed by CBP. Staffed jointly by CBP IA and the Office of Professional Responsibility, JIC is responsible for receiving, documenting, and routing misconduct allegations to the appropriate investigative entity for review to determine whether the allegation can be substantiated. CBP employees or the general public may report allegations to JIC's hotline by e-mail or telephone, to local CBP IA field offices, the DHS Office of Inspector General, or the other law enforcement agencies. Anonymous allegations are also received, documented, and subjected to further inquiry.

The Majority of Arrests against CBP Employees Are Related to Misconduct; Majority of Allegations Occurred at Locations along the Southwest Border

According to CBP's data, incidents of arrests of CBP employees from fiscal years 2005 through 2012 represent less than 1 percent of the entire CBP workforce per fiscal year.[18] During this time period, 144 current or former CBP employees were arrested or indicted for corruption—the majority of which were stationed along the southwest border. In addition, there were 2,170 reported incidents of arrests for misconduct.[19] Allegations against CBPOs and BPAs as a percentage of total on-board personnel remained relatively constant from fiscal years 2006 through 2011 and ranged from serious offenses such as facilitating drug smuggling across the border to administrative delinquencies such as losing an official badge. The majority of allegations made against OFO and USBP employees during this time period were against officers and agents stationed on the southwest U.S. border.

The Majority of Arrests of CBP Employees since Fiscal Year 2005 Are Related to Alleged Misconduct Activities

CBP data indicate that from fiscal year 2005 through fiscal year 2012, the majority of arrests since fiscal year 2005 are related to alleged misconduct activities. A total of 144 current or former CBP employees were arrested or indicted for corruption. In addition, there were 2,170 reported incidents of arrests for misconduct. In both cases, each represents less than 1 percent of the entire CBP workforce per fiscal year. Specifically, in fiscal year 2005, out of 42,409 CBP employees, 27 were arrested or indicted for corruption. In addition, during this time period, there were 190 reported incidents of arrests for misconduct. As of August 2012, when CBP's workforce increased to 60,591, 11 CBP employees were arrested or indicted for corruption, and there were 336 reported incidents of arrests for misconduct. CBP IA defines delinquent

---

[18]CBP collects data on incidents of arrests, indictments, citations, and detainments; for purposes of brevity, we refer to all four categories as "incidents of arrests." According to CBP IA officials, the term "detainments" refers to instances such as those where individuals are intoxicated in public and detained at local facilities until they become sober but do not have an arrest on their record.

[19]CBP does not count the number of employees who have been arrested for misconduct, but rather counts the number of incidents of arrests for misconduct (i.e. one employee may have multiple incidents of arrests for misconduct). For corruption, we have reported the number of employees arrested or indicted for corruption-related activities. Not all arrests result in convictions or disciplinary actions.

activity as either corruption or misconduct. Corruption involves the misuse or abuse of the employee's position, whereas misconduct may not necessarily involve delinquent behavior that is related to the execution of official duties. CBP further categorizes the delinquent behavior into the following categories: (1) non-mission-compromising misconduct, (2) mission-related misconduct, (3) corruption, and (4) mission-compromising corruption. The first category is the only one that is unrelated to the execution of the CBP employee's official duties or authority, and the majority of the incidents of arrests for misconduct (2,153 out of 2,170) since fiscal year 2005 fall in this category. Examples include domestic violence and driving under the influence while off duty. Table 1 provides CBP IA's definitions of the two types of delinquent activity and examples of each category.

Table 1: CBP's Definitions and Examples of Misconduct and Corruption

Misconduct		Corruption	
Non-mission-compromising misconduct Delinquency unrelated to the execution of official duties or one's official authority as a federal law enforcement officer	**Mission-related misconduct** Delinquency related to the execution of official duties or one's official authority as a federal law enforcement officer	**Corruption** Delinquency for personal gain that involved the misuse or abuse of the knowledge, access, or authority granted by virtue of official position	**Mission-compromising corruption** Delinquency for personal gain that involved the misuse or abuse of the knowledge, access, or authority granted by virtue of official position which also violated or facilitated the violation of the laws that CBP enforces
• Driving under the influence/driving while intoxicated • Domestic violence	• Civil rights violations • False imprisonment	• Theft of government property /funds • Fraud • Querying personal associates in a government database	• Alien harboring • Allowing loads of narcotics through a port of entry or checkpoint • Selling immigration documents

Source: GAO analysis of CBP documentation.

From fiscal years 2005 through 2012, a total of 144 employees were arrested or indicted for corruption-related activities, including the smuggling of aliens or drugs, and 125 have been convicted.[20] About 65 percent (93 of 144 arrests) were employees stationed along the

---

[20]As of October 2012, 9 were acquitted or had their cases dismissed, 2 were declined for prosecution, and 8 cases were pending or in pretrial diversion. Of the 125 convictions, 109 were the result of guilty pleas.

southwest border. Our review of documentation on these cases indicates that 103 of the 144 cases were for mission-compromising corruption activities, which are the most severe offenses, such as drug or alien smuggling, bribery, and allowing illegal cargo into the United States. Forty-one of the 144 CBP employees arrested or indicted were charged with other corruption-related activities. According to CBP IA, this category is less severe than mission-compromising corruption and includes offenses such as the theft of government property and querying personal associates in a government database for purposes other than official business. Table 2 provides a breakdown of these arrests by fiscal year.

Table 2: Number of CBP Employees Arrested or Indicted for Corruption-Related Activities, Fiscal Years 2005 through 2012

Fiscal year	2005	2006	2007	2008	2009	2010	2011	2012	Total
Mission-compromising corruption	23	11	8	18	19	8	10	6	**103**
Corruption	4	3	0	3	10	10	5	6	**41**
Corruption subtotal	**27**	**14**	**8**	**21**	**29**	**18**	**15**	**12**	**144**
CBP workforce population (as of August 2012)	42,409	43,545	47,606	52,543	58,600	58,724	59,820	60,591	

Source: GAO analysis of CBP IA data.

Note: Data on CBP employee arrests or indictments are from fiscal year 2005 through 2012. Data on the CBP workforce population for fiscal year 2012 are as of August 2012.

Table 3 outlines the number of incidents of arrests of CBP employees for misconduct for fiscal years 2005 through 2012.

Table 3: Number of Incidents of Arrests of CBP Employees for Misconduct, Fiscal Years 2005 through 2012

Fiscal year	2005	2006	2007	2008	2009	2010	2011	2012	Total
Mission-related misconduct	2	1	1	1	3	1	6	2	**17**
Non-mission compromising misconduct	188	227	225	285	290	303	301	334	**2,153**
Misconduct subtotal	**190**	**228**	**226**	**286**	**293**	**304**	**307**	**336**	**2,170**
CBP workforce population (as of August 2012)	42,409	43,545	47,606	52,543	58,600	58,724	59,820	60,591	

Source: GAO analysis of CBP IA data.

Note: Data on the number of incidents of arrests of CBP employees are from fiscal year 2005 through 2012. Data on the CBP workforce population for fiscal year 2012 are as of August 2012.

Although the total number of corruption convictions (125) is less than 1 percent when compared with CBP's workforce population by fiscal year, CBP officials stated that they are concerned about the negative impact employee corruption cases have on agencywide integrity. For example, the Acting Commissioner of CBP testified that no act of corruption within the agency can or will be tolerated and that acts of corruption compromise CBP's ability to achieve its mission to secure America's borders against all threats while facilitating and expediting legal travel and trade.[21] In particular, there have been a number of cases in which individuals, known as infiltrators, pursued employment at CBP solely to engage in mission-compromising activity. For example, in 2007, a CBPO in El Paso, Texas, was arrested at her duty station at the Paso Del Norte Bridge for conspiracy to import marijuana into the United States from June 2003 to July 2007, and was later convicted and sentenced to 20 years in prison. OFO reported that she may have sought employment with CBP to facilitate drug smuggling. CBP officials view this case as an example of the potential impact of corruption—if the officer had succeeded in facilitating the importation of 5,000 pounds of marijuana per month, this would amount to a total of 240,000 pounds over 4 years with a retail value of $288 million dollars. In another case, a former BPA previously stationed in Comstock, Texas, was arrested in 2008 for conspiracy to possess, with intent to distribute, more than 1,000 kilograms of marijuana. The agent was convicted in 2009 and sentenced to 15 years in prison and ordered to pay a $10,000 fine. CBP is also concerned about employees who may not be infiltrators, but began engaging in corruption-related activities after joining the agency. For example, CBP IA officials stated that some employees may have experienced personal hardships after being hired, such as financial challenges, which made them vulnerable to accepting bribes to engage in corrupt activity. In addition, some employees arrested for corruption had no prior disciplinary actions at the time of their arrests.

---

[21]See Statement of David Aguilar, Acting Commissioner, U.S. Customs and Border Protection, before the Subcommittee on Government Organization, Efficiency, and Financial Management, Committee on Oversight and Government Reform, U.S. House of Representatives. Washington, D.C.: Aug. 1, 2012.

Allegations against CBPOs and BPAs as a Percentage of Total Onboard Personnel Remained Relatively Constant from Fiscal Years 2006 through 2011

According to our analysis of CBP data, from fiscal years 2006 through 2011, a total of 32,290 allegations were made against CBP employees; 90 percent (29,204) were made against CBPOs and BPAs.[22] CBP IA categorizes allegations of misconduct or corruption by varying levels of severity. For example, allegations may range from serious offenses such as facilitating drug smuggling across the border to administrative delinquencies such as losing a badge. CBP allegations of corruption or misconduct are sorted into differing classes depending on the severity of the allegation and whether there is potential for federal prosecution. As table 4 indicates, class 1 allegations comprise the more severe allegations that could lead to federal prosecution, such as drug smuggling or bribery, with classes 2, 3, and 4 representing decreasing levels of severity.

Table 4: Overview of Classes of Allegations of Corruption or Misconduct

Classes of allegations			
Class 1 **Criminal** **(potential federal prosecution)**	**Class 2** **Other criminal or** **serious misconduct**	**Class 3** **Lesser administrative** **violation**	**Class 4** **Information for** **management**
Examples: • Drug smuggling • Alien smuggling • Perjury • Bribery	Examples: • Conflict of interest-association with known criminals/illlegal aliens • Detainee/alien abuse (sexual or physical) • Driving under the influence/driving while intoxicated • Domestic violence	Examples: • Misuse of credentials/ position • Misuse of government database (e.g., querying personal associates)	Examples: • Lost badge/credential (first offense) • Arrest/conviction of family member

Source: GAO analysis of CBP documentation.

Note: Allegations may be reclassified if new information develops during the review of an allegation (e.g., smuggling of a very small amount of drugs may result in a class 2 rather than a class 1 allegation).

Information for management may include notifications such as reporting a lost badge or an arrest of an employee's family member. CBP management will take this information into consideration but may

---

[22]We analyzed allegation data provided by the JIC—CBP's central clearinghouse for receiving, processing, and tracking all allegations of misconduct involving personnel and contractors employed by CBP. Allegations reported to the DHS Office of Inspector General, the Federal Bureau of Investigation, or other law enforcement agencies may not be represented in the data that ar collected by JIC.

determine that the action does not warrant referring the case for further disciplinary action.

Table 5 depicts the number of allegations against CBPOs and BPAs from fiscal years 2006 through 2011. Allegations made against OFO and BP employees as a percentage of the total OFO and USBP workforce remained constant from 12 percent to 14 percent over fiscal years 2006 to 2011.

Table 5: Total Allegations Compared with Total Number of CBPOs and BPAs, Fiscal Years 2006-2011

	2006	2007	2008	2009	2010	2011
Allegations against CBPOs and BPAs	3,554	4,343	4,459	5,352	5,746	5,750
CBPOs and BPAs onboard	30,380	33,377	37,275	41,458	41,245	42,026
Percentage of allegations per number of CBPOs and BPAs (rounded)	12	13	12	13	14	14

Source: GAO analysis of CBP IA data.

Similar to the arrest data, of the total number of allegations made against OFO and USBP employees from fiscal year 2006 to fiscal year 2011—29,204 total allegations—the majority of these allegations were made against officers and agents stationed on the southwest U.S. border. Specifically, there were approximately 19,905 total allegations against CBPOs and BPAs stationed on the southwest border—about 68 percent of total allegations. Approximately 57 percent of all CBPOs and BPAs are stationed along the southwest border. By comparison, during this time period, there were 9,299 allegations made against officers and agents across the rest of CBP's ports of entry and sectors. According to a senior CBP IA official who is responsible for tracking and maintaining CBP allegations data, it is possible that the southwest border region received more allegations, in part, because CBP assigned more employees to the region, many of whom were new, relatively less experienced agents from the hiring increases from fiscal years 2006 through 2011, or were employees on detail to the southwest border region. During this same period, the number of officers and agents and BPAs along the southwest border increased from 15,792 to 24,057. In addition, in each fiscal year from 2006 through 2011, more allegations were made against USBP employees than OFO employees along the southwest border—

allegations against BPAs were about 32 percent higher, on average, than those against CBPOs.

CBP Has Implemented Integrity-Related Controls, but Could Better Assess Screening Tools for Applicants and Incumbent Employees

CBP employs integrity-related controls to mitigate the risk of corruption and misconduct for both applicants and incumbent officers and agents, such as polygraph examinations and random drug testing, respectively. However, CBP does not maintain or track data on which screening tools provided the information that contributed to applicants being deemed unsuitable for hire, making it difficult for CBP to assess the relative effectiveness of these screening tools. In addition, an assessment of the feasibility of expanding the polygraph program to incumbent officers and agents, and consistent implementation of its quality assurance review program for background investigations and periodic reinvestigations, could strengthen CBP's integrity-related controls. OFO and USBP have also implemented controls to help detect and prevent corruption and misconduct; however, additional actions could help improve the effectiveness of OFO's integrity officers.

CBP Employs Controls to Mitigate the Risk of Hiring Potentially Corrupt Officers and Agents, but Does Not Track Data That Can Help Determine the Relative Effectiveness of Screening Tools

CBP has two key controls to screen applicants for CBPO and BPA positions during the hiring process—background investigations and polygraph examinations. Background investigations involve, among other things, a personal interview; a 10-year background check; and an examination of an applicant's criminal, credit, and financial history, according to Office of Personnel Management (OPM) regulations.[23] Polygraph examinations consist of a preinterview, the examination, and a postexamination interview. The Anti-Border Corruption Act of 2010 requires that, as of January 2013, all CBPO and BPA applicants receive polygraph examinations before they are hired.[24] CBP IA officials stated that the agency met the mandated polygraph requirement in October 2012—90 days before the deadline.

PSD considers multiple factors, or a combination thereof, to determine whether an applicant is suitable for employment. PSD officials stated that suitability determinations are based on three adjudication phases: (1) after PSD verifies that each applicant's forms are complete and conducts preliminary law enforcement database and credit checks, (2) after CAD reports the technical results of the polygraph examinations to PSD, and (3) after the completion of the background investigation.[25] PSD is responsible for adjudicating the final polygraph examination results, as

---

[23]On the basis of the sensitivity of the position for which an individual is applying, CBP IA's personnel security officials initiate either a single scope background investigation or a background investigation. The single scope background investigation is required for positions designated as Critical Sensitive National Security. It covers up to 10 years and includes a personal interview and review of the following: employment history, education, residences, references, local law enforcement records, court records, records of former spouse(s), records of spouse or current cohabitant, credit records, and other law enforcement and military records, as applicable. The background investigation is a review of up to 5 years and consists of a personal interview and an examination of the same documents as the single scope background investigation. OPM has delegated authority to CBP to conduct background investigations and make employment suitability determinations for all CBP applicants, contractors, and employees. OPM derives its authority to conduct background investigations from the Executive Order 10450; Executive Order 12968; and Title 5, Code of Federal Regulations, parts 731, 732, and 736.

[24]Pub. L. No. 111-376, § 3, 124 Stat. 4104, 4104-05 (2011).

[25]Historically, CAD initiated the examinations after the background investigations were completed. As of June 2012, CBP began administering polygraph examinations to all new applicants before background investigations are initiated to help rule out unsuitable candidates before expending additional PSD time and resources on costly background investigations. According to CBP IA, the average cost of a polygraph examination is $800, whereas the average cost of a background investigation is about $3,000.

well as reviewing any other information that may be used in determining whether or not applicants are suitable for employment. If, after the final adjudication, there is no derogatory information affecting an applicant's suitability, PSD forwards the final favorable adjudication decision to Human Resources Management, which completes the remainder of the required steps in the hiring process.

Regarding polygraph examinations, CAD has maintained data on the number of polygraph examinations that it administers and the technical results of those examinations since January 2008.[26] CAD officials stated that an applicant technically fails the polygraph examination by receiving a "significant response" on the test or using countermeasures to deceive the test, which is an indicator of deception and results in PSD making a determination that an applicant is unsuitable for hire.[27] Alternatively, an applicant can technically pass the polygraph examination, but admit to past criminal behavior (e.g., admitting to frequent and recent illegal narcotics usage) that would likely render the applicant unsuitable for CBP employment when PSD adjudicates a complete record of CAD's polygraph examination and associated interviews.[28] Table 6 provides our analysis of CAD's data on the 11,149 polygraph examinations administered since 2008, and the technical results of those examinations.

---

[26]CAD administers the polygraph examination program, which includes (1) a pre-examination interview with the applicant, (2) the examination itself, and (3) a postexamination interview. CAD provides a final polygraph examination report to PSD for final adjudication.

[27]Polygraph examinations result in a "significant response" when the applicant displays a physiological response to a question and is ultimately unable to resolve the issue in spite of additional probing during the examination process.

[28]CBP IA defines an admission statement to include any one of the following types of information provided by an applicant: (1) admitting to behavior outside of his self-interest, (2) providing information that was not previously known, (3) admitting to behavior that is relevant to issues that CBP tests, and/or (4) admitting information that was not relevant to determining suitability for employment.

Table 6: Technical Results of Polygraph Examinations, January 2008 to August 2012

Fiscal year	Total tests conducted	Failed tests[a]	Failure rate	Passed tests	Passed rate	Inconclusive	Inconclusive rate
2008 (January through September)	505	158	31%	292	58%	55	11%
2009	2,047	733	36%	1,031	50%	283	14%
2010	2,069	975	47%	907	44%	187	9%
2011	2,688	1,361	51%	978	36%	349	13%
2012 (through August 7, 2012)	3,840	1,917	50%	1,255	33%	668	17%
Total	**11,149**	**5,144**	**46%**	**4,463**	**40%**	**1,542**	**14%**

Source: GAO analysis of CBP IA data.

Note: Of the 11,149 examinations, 859 were retests (i.e., an applicant had to retake the examination usually because of an initial inconclusive result.) Retest results were proportionally similar to the results for all polygraph examinations.

[a]Failed test refers to a test with a significant response and/or a no opinion or no opinion-counter measure. "No opinion" means that no exam was administered or no viable exam could be collected (usually because of an applicant not appearing for a scheduled exam). A "no opinion-counter measure" represents an attempt by the applicant to deceive the exam.

In addition to the technical examination results, CAD maintains documentation on admissions that applicants reveal during the polygraph examination process. Applicants have admitted to a range of criminal activity from plans to gain employment with the agency in order to further illicit activities, such as drug smuggling to excessive illegal drug use. For example, one applicant admitted that his brother-in-law, a known Mexican drug smuggler, asked him to use employment with CBP to facilitate cocaine smuggling. Another applicant admitted to using marijuana 9,000 times, including the night before the polygraph examination; cocaine 30 to 40 times; hallucinogenic mushrooms 15 times; and ecstasy about 50 times. CBP IA officials stated that admissions such as these highlight the importance of the polygraph examination to help identify these types of behaviors in applicants before they are hired for CBP employment. CBP IA officials stated that the polygraph examination is the key investigative tool in the agency's integrity program because it can help identify whether applicants have misled background investigators regarding previous criminal histories or misconduct issues.

PSD is responsible for maintaining data on its final suitability determinations—whether or not it determines that applicants are suitable for hire. However, CBP IA does not have a mechanism to track and maintain data on which of its screening tools (e.g., background information or polygraph examination) provided the information that PSD used to determine that applicants were not suitable for hire, making it difficult for CBP IA to assess the relative effectiveness of its various screening tools. For example, if 100 applicants technically pass a polygraph examination, but 60 of these applicants are ultimately found unsuitable for hire, CBP IA does not have data to indicate if the applicants were found unsuitable based on admissions during the polygraph examination, derogatory information collected by background investigators, a combination of this information, or on the basis of other screening tools. PSD officials stated that they do not have the data needed to assess the effectiveness of screening tools because of limitations in PSD's information management system, the Integrated Security Management System (ISMS), which is not designed to collect data on the source of the information (e.g., background information, polygraph examination) and the results used to determine whether an applicant is deemed suitable for hire.[29] CBP IA's Assistant Commissioner and other senior staff stated that maintaining these data on an ongoing basis would be useful in managing CBP IA's programs.

Standards for Internal Control in the Federal Government states that program managers need operational data to determine whether they are meeting their goals for accountability for effective and efficient use of resources. Moreover, the standards state that pertinent information should be identified, captured, and distributed in a form and time frame that permits managers to perform their duties efficiently. The standards also require that all transactions be clearly documented in a manner that is complete and accurate in order to be useful for managers and others involved in evaluating operations.[30] Maintaining and tracking data on which screening tools provide information that contributes to PSD determining that an applicant is not suitable for hire could better position CBP IA to gauge the effectiveness of each tool and the extent to which the tools are meeting their intended goals for screening applicants for hire.

---

[29]PSD uses DHS's Integrated Security Management System (ISMS) to track data on its adjudications. CBP IA began using ISMS, as required by DHS, in fiscal year 2010.

[30]GAO/AIMD-00-21.3.1.

CBP Has Tools for Screening Incumbent Officers and Agents

CBP has two key controls for incumbent employees—random drug testing and periodic reinvestigations—to ensure the continued integrity of the CBPOs and BPAs. CBP is required to conduct random drug tests on an annual basis for at least 10 percent of the employees in designated positions,[31] including CBPOs and BPAs, to help ensure employees who hold positions in the area of law enforcement or public trust refrain from the use of illegal drugs while on or off duty.[32] According to CBP data for fiscal years 2009 through 2011, more than 99 percent of the 15,565 random drug tests conducted on CBP employees were negative. CBP officials stated that actions against those with positive results ranged from voluntary resignation to removal. In September 2012, Human Resource Management officials told us that DHS was in the process of reviewing drug-free workplace programs across the department and that CBP was coordinating with DHS's drug-free workforce program. Changes under consideration for DHS's program include eliminating the 2-hour advance notice that employees currently receive before they are required to provide a urinalysis sample, which human resource officials stated could help reduce the possibility of CBP employees potentially engaging in efforts to dilute the results of the tests.

In addition, CBP policy states that all CBPOs and BPAs are subject to a reinvestigation every 5 years to ensure continued suitability for employment.[33] According to CBP IA officials, reinvestigations are a key control for monitoring incumbent officers and agents, particularly for those employees who were hired in the past without a polygraph examination.[34]

---

[31]Human Resources Management administers the CBP Federal Drug Free Workplace Program as is mandated by Executive Order 12564. Tested designated positions include sensitive federal positions in the area of law enforcement and public trust such as CBPOs and BPAs.

[32]CBP also conducts urinalysis tests based on reasonable suspicion or in the aftermath of an accident or in other instances. Grounds for reasonable suspicion tests include, among other things, observable phenomena, such as direct observation of drug use or possession and/or the physical symptoms of being under the influence of a drug, a pattern of abnormal conduct or erratic behavior, or an arrest or conviction for a drug-related offense. CBP conducted five reasonable suspicion tests from fiscal years 2009 to 2011.

[33]CBP policies allows for reinvestigations to be initiated outside of the standard 5-year cycle. As of July 2012, CBP has not conducted any periodic reinvestigations outside of the normal cycle, according to CBP IA officials.

[34]As of October 2012, CBP requires all incoming CBPO and BPA applicants to receive a polygraph examination. However, PSD began screening some applicants with a polygraph examination beginning in 2008.

CBP IA officials stated that they conducted few periodic reinvestigations during fiscal years 2006 to 2010 because resources were focused on meeting mandated hiring goals.[35] Thus, CBP IA accumulated a backlog of 15,197 periodic reinvestigations as of 2010. To help address this backlog, the Anti-Border Corruption Act of 2010 required CBP to initiate all outstanding periodic reinvestigations within 180 days of the enactment of the law, or July 3, 2011.[36] As of September 2012, CBP IA had initiated 100 percent, and had completed 99 percent (15,027 of 15,197) of the outstanding reinvestigations from the backlog. According to CBP IA officials, 13,968 of the reinvestigations that were completed as of September 2012 have been adjudicated favorably, and CBP officials stated that they had referred three additional cases to the Office of Labor and Employee Relations for possible disciplinary action.[37] CBP IA data indicate, however, that about 62 percent of the favorably adjudicated reinvestigations initially identified some type of issue, such as criminal or dishonest conduct or illegal drug use, which required further review during the adjudication process. According to CBP IA officials, PSD adjudicators mitigated these issues and determined that they did not warrant any referrals to labor and employee relations officials for disciplinary actions.

CBP Has Not Assessed the Feasibility of Expanding Its Polygraph Program to Incumbent Officers and Agents

CBP IA officials stated that they are considering implementing a polygraph requirement for incumbent employees; however, CBP has not yet assessed the feasibility of expanding the program beyond applicants. In May 2012, CBP's Acting Deputy Commissioner testified that the agency is considering whether and how to subject incumbent officers and agents to polygraph examinations.[38] CBP IA officials and supervisory CBPOs and BPAs that we interviewed at all four of the locations we visited expressed

---

[35]In fiscal years 2011 and 2012, appropriations acts provided that the Border Patrol was to maintain an active duty presence of no fewer than 21,370 agents protecting the border of the United States. Department of Defense and Full-Year Continuing Appropriations Act, 2011, div. B, tit. VI, § 1608, Pub. L. No. 112-10, 125 Stat. 38, 140; Consolidated Appropriations Act, 2012, div. D, tit. II, Pub. L. No. 112-74, 125 Stat. 786, 945-46 (2011).

[36]Pub. L. No. 111-376, § 3, 124 Stat. 4104, 4104-05 (2011).

[37]The Office of Labor and Employee Relations is the authority within CBP for management of labor and employee relations activities.

[38]Statement of Thomas Winkowski, Acting Deputy Commissioner, U.S. Customs and Border Protection, before the Subcommittee on Oversight, Investigations, and Management, Committee on Homeland Security, U.S. House of Representatives. Washington, D.C.: May 17, 2012.

concerns about the suitability of the officers and agents hired during the surges because most of these officers and agents did not take a polygraph examination. CBP IA's Assistant Commissioner also stated that he supports a periodic polygraph requirement for incumbent officers because of the breadth and volume of derogatory information that applicants have provided during the polygraph examinations. The Assistant Commissioner and other senior CBP officials stated that they have begun to consider various factors related to expanding polygraph examinations to incumbent officers and agents in CBP. However, CBP has not yet fully assessed the costs and benefits of implementing polygraph examinations on incumbent officers and agents, as well as other factors that may affect the agency's efforts to expand the program. For example:

- **Costs.** In September 2012, CBP IA officials told us that they had not fully examined the costs associated with different options for expanding the polygraph examination requirement to incumbent employees. To test 5 percent of current eligible law enforcement employees (about 45,000 officer and agents), for example, equates to 2,250 polygraph examinations annually, according to CBP IA. Testing 20 percent of eligible employees each year, by comparison, equates to 9,000 polygraph examinations annually. CBP IA preliminarily identified some costs based on the average cost per polygraph examination (about $800); however, it has not completed analyses of other costs associated with testing incumbent employees, including those associated with mission support specialists, adjudicators, and supervisors who would need to be hired and trained to conduct the examinations. In October 2012, CBP IA officials stated that there would be further costs associated with training polygraph examiners— approximately $250,000 per examiner. CBP has not determined the full costs associated with expanding polygraph examinations to incumbent employees to help assess the feasibility of various options for expansion.

- **Authority and ability to polygraph incumbents.** According to OPM requirements, to conduct polygraph examinations on current employees, CBP would need to request and obtain approval from OPM. As of September 2012, CBP had not yet sought approval from OPM to conduct polygraph examinations on incumbent employees because CBP's senior leadership had not completed internal discussions about how and when to seek this approval. In addition, CBP officials identified other factors that the agency has not yet assessed, which could affect the feasibility of conducting polygraph examinations on incumbent employees. These factors include the need to assess how the agency will use the results of incumbent employees' polygraphs and whether these options are subject to negotiation with the labor unions that represent CBPOs and BPAs. For example, according to CBP officials, it might be necessary to negotiate with the unions as to what disciplinary action could be taken based on the possible outcomes of the examination, including the test results themselves and any admissions of illegal activity or misconduct made by the employee during the examination.

- **Frequency or number of polygraph examinations to be conducted.** According to the CBP IA Assistant Commissioner, the agency has identified possible options for how frequently to implement polygraph examinations for incumbent employees or for what population to conduct the examinations. For example, possible options include conducting polygraph examinations on a random sample of incumbent employees each year (e.g., 5 percent or 20 percent of eligible employees each year), or conducting the examinations based on reasonable suspicion of finding derogatory information. CBP IA officials stated that testing incumbent employees on a random basis could have a deterrent effect by causing some employees to cease their corrupt behavior, and dissuading other employees from becoming involved in corrupt behavior. Although CBP has identified possible options for how frequently to implement polygraph examinations for incumbent employees or for what population to conduct the examinations, CBP officials stated that they have not assessed the feasibility of implementing these options, particularly in light of their relative costs and benefits.

Standard practices for project management call for the feasibility of programs to be considered early on.[39] Moreover, standard practices for project management state that specific desired outcomes or results should be conceptualized, defined, and documented as part of a road map.[40]

CBP has not fully assessed the feasibility of expanding the polygraph program to incumbent officers and agents, in accordance with standard

---

[39]See GAO, *Feasibility and Cost-Benefit Analysis Would Assist DHS and Congress in Assessing and Implementing the Requirement to Scan 100 Percent of U.S.-Bound Containers*, GAO-10-12 (Washington, D.C.: Oct. 30, 2009).

[40]Project Management Institute, *The Standard for Program Management*, second edition© (Newton Square, Pa., 2006, updated 2008).

practices for project management, including assessing all of the associated costs and benefits, options for how the agency will use the results of the examinations, and the trade-offs associated with testing incumbent officers and agents at various frequencies. In October 2012, the CBP IA Assistant Commissioner stated that the agency has begun to discuss options with senior agency officials for expanding its polygraph program. He and other senior CBP IA officials acknowledged that his office had not yet fully assessed the various factors that might affect the feasibility of expanding the polygraph program and agreed that such an assessment would be useful in discussions with CBP senior management. Assessing the feasibility of expanding periodic polygraphs early on in its planning efforts, consistent with standard practices, could help CBP determine how to best achieve its goal of strengthening integrity-related controls over incumbent CBPOs and BPAs.

CBP IA Could Benefit from Implementing Its Quality Assurance Program for Initial Background and Periodic Reinvestigations

A senior PSD official stated that PSD has not implemented a quality assurance program at the level desired because it has prioritized its resources in recent years to address hiring goals and the mandated requirements to clear the backlog of reinvestigations.[41] PSD established a quality assurance program in 2008 to help ensure that proper policies and procedures are followed during the course of the preemployment background investigations and incumbent employee reinvestigations. As part of this program, PSD is to (1) review, on a monthly basis, no more than 5 percent of all completed investigations to ensure the quality and timeliness of the investigations and to identify any deficiencies in the investigation process, and (2) report the findings or deficiencies in a standardized checklist so that corrective action can be taken, if necessary. As of September 2012, PSD officials stated that they have not consistently completed the monthly checks, as required by the quality assurance program, because they have prioritized their resources to screen applicants to meet CBP's hiring goals. PSD officials stated that they have performed some of the required checks since 2008. However, PSD officials could not provide data on how many checks were conducted or when the checks were conducted because they did not retain the results of the checks on the required checklists. In addition,

---

[41]CAD adheres to a separate quality assurance program that is administered by the National Center for Credibility Assessment, which evaluates CAD's compliance with established policies and procedures for polygraph programs within the federal government.

CBP IA officials stated that they had performed 16 quality reviews on an ad hoc basis outside of the monthly checks from fiscal years 2008 through 2010. CBP IA documented the results of these ad hoc checks, which did not identify significant deficiencies according to officials.

Standards for Internal Control in the Federal Government provides guidance on the importance of evaluating the effectiveness of controls and ensuring that the findings of audits and other reviews are promptly resolved and evaluated within established time frames so that all actions that correct or otherwise resolve the matters have been brought to management's attention. The standards also state that all transactions and other significant events need to be clearly documented, and the documentation should be readily available for examination. Senior CBP IA officials stated that a quality assurance program is an integral part of their overall applicant screening efforts, and they stated that it is critical for CBP IA to identify and leverage resources to ensure that the quality assurance program is fully implemented on a consistent basis. Without a quality review program that is implemented and documented on a consistent basis, it is difficult to determine the extent to which deficiencies, if any, exist in the investigation and adjudication process and whether individuals that are unsuitable for employment are attempting to find employment with CBP. As a result, it is difficult for CBP to provide reasonable assurance that cases have been investigated and adjudicated properly and that corruption risk to the agency is mitigated accordingly.

OFO and USBP Have Developed Integrity-Related Controls; OFO Could Benefit from Clarifying the Roles and Responsibilities of Its Integrity Officers

In addition to CBP's screening tools for applicants and incumbent employees, OFO and USBP have developed controls to help mitigate the risk of potential CBPO and BPA corruption and misconduct (see table 7).[42] For example, OFO has been able to use upgraded technology at ports of entry to help prevent and detect possible officer misconduct and to monitor officers' activities while on duty. USBP established a policy that limits the use of portable electronic devices while on duty to mitigate the risks of agents potentially organizing illegal border crossings.

---

[42]OFO and BP have also developed various policies, musters, training courses, and other documents outlining officers' and agents' integrity-related responsibilities related to accessing U.S. government law enforcement systems, inappropriate associations with known or suspected criminals, processing of family or close associates, among other things.

Table 7: Key OFO and USBP Integrity-Related Controls

OFO	USBP
Analytical Management Systems and Control Office (AMSCO): AMSCO, established in 2009, analyzes border crossing and other system data to help identify normal patterns of behavior versus anomalies that may be indicative of integrity issues. According to CBP officials, data from AMSCO have proved beneficial in ongoing corruption investigations and also assist in the development of potential leads against possible corrupt CBP employees. In addition, AMSCO has been useful in identifying additional training needs or system adjustments for CBPOs.	**AMSCO:** In 2012, USBP assigned two agents to AMSCO to learn from OFO and develop, as feasible, similar testing of available USBP data.
Red Flag: Computerized system that sends electronic alerts via handheld devices to CBP supervisors at ports of entry if individual officers have potentially not followed standard policies. As of August 2012, Red Flag technology has been implemented at 12 ports of entry along the southwest border, and OFO officials stated that they plan to extend the technology to other ports in fiscal year 2013.	**Portable electronic devices:** BPAs are allowed limited use of personal electronic devices while on duty if usage does not interfere with official business. The policy also prohibits sensitive information on personal global positioning systems without supervisory approval and discourages the use of wireless communications, other than sector communications systems, to transmit official business. USBP instituted this policy to help mitigate the risks that BPAs alone on patrol could organize illegal border crossings or smuggling activities.
Unscheduled lane rotations: During primary inspection at land ports, OFO's first-line supervisors may require CBPOs to change lane assignments immediately and without the officers' prior knowledge to help mitigate the risk of officers having previously informed drug or human smugglers of the lane in which they would be working.	**Agent assignment restrictions:** USBP trainees are prohibited from being initially assigned within a 100-mile radius of their preemployment home of record based on a USBP analysis of former USBP employees who have been arrested for alleged corruption, which concluded that 75 percent of these individuals had been assigned near their preemployment home of record and therefore placed in an environment where they were more likely to face pressure from friends and family to engage in illicit activities such as smuggling.
Unscheduled work locations: Advanced details about employee work locations are withheld to mitigate risk of officers coordinating illegal activity more easily with those individuals who are seeking to smuggle illicit goods or aliens into the country.	

Source: GAO analysis of OFO and USBP information.

Senior USBP officials stated that its agents operate in an environment that does not lend itself to the types of technological controls, such as Red Flag, that OFO has implemented at the ports of entry, which are more confined and predictable environments than Border Patrol environments. For example, BPAs are required to patrol miles of terrain that may be inaccessible to radio coverage by supervisors at the sector offices. CBPOs operate in more controlled space at U.S. ports of entry as opposed to the open terrain across USBP sectors. Nevertheless, USBP officials stated that they are working with AMSCO and CBP IA to identify innovative ways that technology might be used to assist USBP in mitigating the risk of corruption along the border.

In addition, in 2009, OFO established the integrity officer position to provide an additional control within the individual field offices. As of August 2012, there were 19 integrity officers across OFO's 20 field offices; there were 5 officers across the 4 field offices on the southwest border. Integrity officers monitor integrity-related controls, including the Red Flag system and video surveillance cameras. Integrity officers also perform data analyses and provide operational support to criminal and administrative investigations against OFO employees. However, CBP IA officials stated that OFO has not consistently coordinated the integrity officer program with CBP IA, which is the designated lead for all integrity-related matters within CBP. According to a CBP directive, entities within CBP, such as OFO, that are engaged in integrity-related activities must coordinate with CBP IA to ensure organizational awareness and prevent investigative conflicts.[43] CBP IA officials stated that although they are aware of the Integrity Officer program, they expressed concerns that the roles and responsibilities of these officers may not be clearly articulated and thus could result in potential problems, such as jeopardizing ongoing investigations.

In August 2012, CBP's Acting Commissioner testified that integrity officers participate in local corruption task forces, committees, and working groups, and collaborate with various federal law enforcement agencies to provide assistance in operational inquiries, research, and analysis to assist in the detection and deterrence of corruption and misconduct.[44] OFO's documentation on integrity officers' duties does not provide specific details about how they are to provide assistance to the investigative entities. The documentation states that they are to "assist with operational inquiries" and serve as technical experts on matters related to "inspections, intelligence, analysis, examination and enforcement" activities. However, there are differences in how the integrity officers have interpreted OFO's guidance on their roles and

---

[43]CBP Directive 2130-016.

[44]See Statement of David Aguilar, Acting Commissioner, U.S. Customs and Border Protection, before the Subcommittee on Government Organization, Efficiency, and Financial Management, Committee on Oversight and Government Reform, U.S. House of Representatives. Washington, D.C.: Aug. 1, 2012.

responsibilities, including the definition of assisting with operational inquiries. For example, in our meetings with 4 of the integrity officers along the southwest border, we found that 3 defined their role to include active participation in investigations of allegations of misconduct and corruption against OFO employees. At one location we visited, the integrity officer stated that he had created an online social media profile under an assumed name to connect with CBP employees at his port of entry, one of whom was under investigation—an activity that the OFO Program Manager, senior OFO officials, and CBP IA officials acknowledged was beyond the scope of the intended role of the integrity officer position. Further, one integrity officer indicated that his role includes a right to "fully investigate" CBP employees, while another interpreted his role to be limited to conducting data analysis.

CBP IA officials stated that integrity officers are not authorized to conduct investigations nor are they trained to do so. Differences in integrity officers' activities across field locations could be justified given the variances at each port of entry. CBP IA officials expressed concerns, however, that the integrity officers may be overstepping their roles by inserting themselves into ongoing investigations, which could potentially disrupt or jeopardize ongoing investigations because they could unknowingly compromise the independence of an investigation or interview. OFO's Acting Assistant Commissioner and the integrity officer program manager acknowledged that it would be useful to further clarify integrity officers' duties to avoid any conflicts with ongoing investigations and ensure that the officers were approaching their duties more consistently. Clear roles and responsibilities for integrity officers developed in consultation with key stakeholders such as CBP IA, and a mechanism that monitors the implementation of those roles and responsibilities, could help OFO ensure that the program is operating effectively and, in particular, in coordination with the appropriate stakeholders like CBP IA.

An Agencywide Strategy and Lessons Learned Analyses Could Help Guide CBP Integrity-Related Efforts

CBP has not developed a comprehensive integrity strategy to encompass all CBP components' initiatives. Further, CBP has not completed some postcorruption analyses on employees convicted of corruption since October 2004, missing opportunities to gain lessons learned to enhance policies, procedures, and controls.

CBP Is Developing an Integrity Strategy, but Does Not Have Target Timelines for Its Completion and Implementation

CBP has not completed an integrity strategy that encompasses the activities of CBP components that have integrity initiatives under way, including CBP IA, OFO, and USBP, as called for in the CBP Fiscal Year 2009-2014 Strategic Plan.[45] Specifically, CBP's Strategic Plan states that it will deploy a comprehensive integrity strategy that integrates prevention, detection, and investigation. Further, a 2008 CBP directive states that CBP IA is responsible for developing and implementing CBP's comprehensive integrity strategy to prevent, detect, and investigate all threats to the integrity of CBP.[46] We have previously reported that developing effective strategies can help ensure successful implementation of agencywide undertakings where multiple entities are involved, such as CBP integrity-related efforts.[47] Elements of an effective strategy include, among others, (1) identifying the purpose, scope, and particular problems and threats the strategy is directed toward; (2) establishing goals, subordinate objectives and activities, priorities, timelines, and performance measures; (3) defining costs, benefits, and

---

[45]U.S. Customs and Border Protection. *Secure Borders, Safe Travel, Legal Trade: U.S. Customs and Border Protection Fiscal Year 2009-2014 Strategic Plan.* Washington, D.C.: July 2009.

[46]CBP Directive 2130-016.

[47]GAO, *Efforts to Develop a National Biosurveillance Capability Need a National Strategy and a Designated Leader*, GAO-10-645 (Washington, D.C.: June 30, 2010) and GAO, *National Capital Region: 2010 Strategic Plan is Generally Consistent with Characteristics of Effective Strategies*, GAO-12-276T (Washington, D.C.: Dec. 7, 2011).

resource and investment needs; and (4) delineating roles and responsibilities.[48]

CBP has efforts under way to help coordinate the various components' integrity-related initiatives, but these efforts have not fully addressed the elements of a comprehensive integrity strategy that integrates prevention, detection, and investigative initiatives for all CBP components. First, CBP IA developed a fiscal year 2010-2015 strategic implementation plan to guide its programs that aim to prevent, detect, and respond to corruption in CBP's workforce. While CBP IA's implementation plan sets goals and objectives and assigning roles and responsibilities for CBP IA's programs, it does not address the goals or resources necessary across other components. Second, CBP convened the Integrity Integrated Policy Coordination Committee (IPCC) in March 2011 to provide a forum to discuss integrity-related issues among representative members from CBP component agencies and other stakeholders.[49] IPCC provides recommendations to CBP's Commissioner to improve integrity programs and initiatives, but does not have the authority provided to CBP IA in the 2008 directive to implement an agencywide integrity strategy or assign roles and responsibilities nor has it defined resource and investment needs for a comprehensive integrity strategy. Last, at the component level, USBP established an Integrity Advisory Committee in 2008 to disseminate integrity and ethics information throughout the sectors and provide recommendations to help combat corruption and promote integrity within the workforce. In addition, USBP established local

---

[48]GAO, *Combating Terrorism: Evaluation of Selected Characteristics in National Strategies Related to Terrorism,* GAO-04-408T (Washington, D.C.: Feb. 3, 2004). Another element of effective strategies that we identified was integration and implementation, which addresses how a strategy relates to other strategies' goals, objectives, and activities, and to subordinate levels of government and their plans to implement the strategy. We determined that this element was not relevant to the scope of our review, which was limited to CBP's integrity programs and strategy and not its integration with integrity activities of other DHS components.

[49]CBP convened the IPCC in 2011 as a forum to discuss integrity-related issues and ideas and to share best practices among the members. IPCC is responsible for facilitating integrity-related operations of individual offices within CBP as a deliberative body. In particular, IPCC was tasked with making recommendations to address the results of an integrity study conducted by the Homeland Security Studies and Analysis Institute. The IPCC is composed of representatives from CBP IA, OFO, USBP, Human Resources Management, and Labor and Employee Relations, among others. See Homeland Security Studies and Analysis Institute, *U.S. Customs and Border Protection Workforce Integrity Study.* Dec. 15, 2011.

committees in selected sectors, including along the southwest border, to establish training and guidance to help BPAs and reinforce concepts such as professional behavior and ethical decision making. OFO established an Integrity Committee to review misconduct and corruption data related to OFO employees, identify potential trends, and develop integrity initiatives to address any concerns. Although CBP IA has a strategic implementation plan for its activities and officials told us that these integrity coordination committees have been useful as forums for sharing information about the components' respective integrity-related initiatives, CBP has not yet developed and deployed an agencywide integrity strategy.

During the course of our review, CBP IA began drafting an integrity strategy for approval by the components and CBP's senior management, in accordance with CBP's *Fiscal Year 2009-2014 Strategic Plan*. CBP IA officials stated that a comprehensive strategy is important because it would help guide CBP integrity efforts and can, in turn, lead to specific objectives and activities, better allocation and management of resources, and clarification of roles and responsibilities. A 2011 workforce integrity study commissioned by CBP recommended that CBP develop a comprehensive integrity strategy and concluded that without such a strategy, there is potential for inconsistent efforts, conflicting roles and responsibilities, and unintended redundancies.[50] However, CBP IA's Assistant Commissioner stated that, as of September 2012, his office had not developed timelines for completing and implementing the agencywide integrity strategy and has not been able to finalize the draft, in accordance with the *Fiscal Year 2009-2014 Strategic Plan*. He indicated that that there has been significant cultural resistance among some CBP component entities in acknowledging CBP IA's authority and responsibility for overseeing the implementation of all CBP integrity-related activities. Program management standards state that successful execution of any program includes developing plans that include a timeline for program deliverables.[51] Without target timelines, it will be difficult for CBP to monitor progress made toward the development and implementation of an agencywide strategy. Further, it is too soon for us to

---

[50]Homeland Security Studies and Analysis Institute, *U.S. Customs and Border Protection Workforce Integrity Study*. Dec. 15, 2011.

[51]Project Management Institute, *The Standard for Program Management*, second edition © (Newton Square, Pa., 2006, updated 2008).

determine if the final strategy will meet the key elements of an effective strategy that encompasses CBP-wide integrity stakeholders' goals, milestones, performance measures, resource needs, and roles and responsibilities. A strategy that includes these elements could help better position CBP to provide oversight and coordination of integrity initiatives occurring across the agency.

CBP Has Not Yet Completed Analyses of Prior Cases of Corruption

CBP has not completed some analyses of some cases in which CBPOs and BPAs were convicted of corruption-related charges. Such analyses could provide CBP with information to better identify corruption or misconduct risks to the workforce or modify existing policies, procedures, and controls to better detect or prevent possible corrupt activities on the part of CBPOs and BPAs. In 2007, OFO directed relevant managers to complete postcorruption analysis reports for each employee convicted for corruption. In 2011, USBP began requiring that these reports be completed after the conviction of any USBP employee for corruption. The reports are to include information such as how the employee committed the corrupt activity, and provide, among other things, recommendations on how USBP and OFO could improve policies, procedures, and controls to prevent or detect similar corruption in the future. For example, according to an OFO Director, several reports stated that the use of personal cell phones helped facilitate and coordinate drug smuggling efforts. As a result of these analyses, OFO implemented a restriction on the use of personal cell phones while on duty.

As of October 2012, OFO has completed about 66 percent of the total postcorruption analysis reports on OFO employees convicted since October 2004 (47 of 71 total convictions). OFO's Incident Management Division Director stated that OFO had not completed the remaining reports because some convictions occurred prior to the 2007 OFO directive or because the convictions had not been published on CBP IA's internal website—a point that informs OFO when it has 30 days to complete the report.[52] USBP has completed about 4 percent of postcorruption anlaysis reports on USBP employees convicted since October 2004 (2 of 45 total convictions). USBP was instructed to complete postcorruption analysis reports in August 2011, and USBP

---

[52]CBP's "Trust Betrayed" internal website lists examples of behavior that CBP states betrays the conduct expected of employees, and includes details of criminal prosecutions.

officials stated that the agency does not have plans to complete analyses for convictions before August 2011 because CBP IA is reviewing these cases as part of a study to analyze behavioral traits among corrupt employees. However, CBP IA's study does not substitute for postcorruption analysis reports because for this study, CBP IA researchers are exploring the convicted employees' thinking and behavior to gain insights into the motives behind the betrayal of trust, how the activity originated, and how they carried out the illegal activity. The postcorruption reports, however, may go beyond this type of analysis and also may aim to identify deficiencies in port or sector processes that may have fostered or permitted corruption and to produce recommendations specific to enhancing USBP policies, procedures, or controls. A USBP Deputy Chief acknowledged that completing the remaining reports could be beneficial to understanding any trends or patterns of behavior among BPAs convicted of corruption. In some cases, OFO and USBP officials stated that it may be difficult to complete postcorruption analysis reports for older convictions, as witnesses and other information on the corruption-related activities may no longer be available.

Standards for Internal Control in the Federal Government provides guidance on the importance of identifying and analyzing risks, and using that information to make decisions.[53] These standards address various aspects of internal control that should be continuous, built-in components of organizational operations. One internal control standard, risk assessment, calls for identifying and analyzing risks that agencies face from internal and external sources and deciding what actions should be taken to manage these risks. The standards indicate that conditions governing risk continually change and periodic updates are required to ensure that risk information, such as vulnerabilities in the program, remains current and relevant. Information collected through periodic reviews, as well as daily operations, can inform the analysis and assessment of risk. Complete and timely information from postcorruption analysis reports of all convictions could assist USBP and OFO management in obtaining and sharing lessons learned to enhance integrity-related policies, procedures, and controls throughout CBP.

---

[53]GAO/AIMD-00-21.3.1.

Conclusions

Data indicate that the overwhelming majority of CBP employees adhere to the agency's integrity standards; however, a small minority have been convicted of engaging in corruption due, in part, to the increasing pressure from drug-trafficking and other transnational criminal organizations that are targeting CBPOs and BPAs, particularly along the southwest U.S. border. The Acting Commissioner of CBP testified that no act of corruption within the agency can or will be tolerated and that acts of corruption compromise CBP's ability to achieve its mission to secure America's borders against all threats while facilitating and expediting legal travel and trade. Strategic and continuous monitoring of operational vulnerabilities is important given the shifting tactics of drug-trafficking organizations seeking to infiltrate the agency. Therefore, CBP has taken steps to mitigate the risk of misconduct and corruption among incoming CBPOs and BPAs by implementing controls during the preemployment screening process. However, tracking and maintaining data on the results of its screening tools for applicants, a feasibility assessment for potential expansion of polygraph requirements, and a robust quality assurance program for background investigations and periodic reinvestigations that ensures reviews are consistently conducted and documented could better position CBP to mitigate risk of employee corruption. In addition, clear roles and responsibilities for OFO's integrity officers developed in coordination with appropriate stakeholders such as CBP IA could help CBP ensure that the program is operating effectively. Moreover, establishing a target time frame for completing a comprehensive integrity strategy could help CBP ensure sufficient progress toward its development and implementation. In addition, completed, postcorruption analysis reports of former CBP employees who have been arrested for corruption could better position CBP to implement any lessons learned from these cases.

Recommendations for Executive Action

To enhance CBP's efforts to mitigate the risk of corruption and misconduct among CBPOs and BPAs, we recommend that the CBP commissioner take the following seven actions:

- develop a mechanism to maintain and track data on the sources of information (e.g., background investigation or polygraph examination admissions) that PSD uses to determine what applicants are not suitable for hire to help CBP IA assess the effectiveness of its applicant screening tools;
- assess the feasibility of expanding the polygraph program to incumbent CBPOs and BPAs, including the associated costs and benefits, options for how the agency will use the results of the

examinations, and the trade-offs associated with testing incumbent officers and agents at various frequencies;

- conduct quality assurance reviews of CBP IA's adjudications of background investigations and periodic reinvestigations, as required in PSD's quality assurance program;
- establish a process to fully document, as required, any deficiencies identified through PSD's quality assurance reviews;
- develop detailed guidance within OFO on the roles and responsibilities for integrity officers, in consultation with appropriate stakeholders such as CBP IA;
- set target timelines for completing and implementing a comprehensive integrity strategy; and,
- complete OFO and USBP postcorruption analysis reports for all CBPOs and BPAs who have been convicted of corruption-related activities, to the extent that information is available.

Agency Comments and Our Evaluation

We provided a draft of this report to DHS for its review and comment. DHS provided written comments, which are reproduced in full in appendix II. DHS concurred with all seven recommendations and described actions under way or plans to address them. DHS also discussed concerns it had with periodically polygraphing incumbent law enforcement officers.

With regard to our first recommendation, DHS concurred and indicated that by March 31, 2013, CBP expects to collect data on the impact of the polygraph examination regarding the outcome of CBP applicant suitability adjudications and undertake steps to ensure data reliability across various CBP personnel security databases.

With regard to the second recommendation, while DHS concurred, it reported possible adverse impacts associated with periodically polygraphing incumbent law enforcement officers. Specifically, DHS noted that doing so could adversely affect CBP resources without additional resources to implement the requirement. While we understand DHS's concerns, we did not recommend that CBP expand its polygraph program to incumbent employees; rather, we recommended that CBP assess the feasibility of expanding polygraph examinations to incumbent CBPOs and BPAs. Thus, concerns such as these could be considered in conducting its feasibility assessment. As we reported, assessing the feasibility of expanding periodic polygraphs early on in its planning efforts could help CBP determine how to best achieve its goal of strengthening integrity-related controls over incumbent CBPOs and BPAs. In addition, DHS noted that expanding the polygraph program to incumbent employees would be contingent on approval from OPM and may encounter resistance from unions representing CBP's employees who may view it as a potential change to the conditions of their employment. As noted in the report, these are important factors CBP could consider in assessing the feasibility of expanding the polygraph program.

With regard to the other five recommendations, DHS concurred and indicated that CBP will work to strengthen its current quality assurance processes and develop a process to document deficiencies identified through quality reviews; develop detailed guidance on the duties, roles, and responsibilities of integrity officers; complete a comprehensive integrity strategy; and develop postcorruption analysis reports for any convictions that do not currently have such reports. DHS estimates that it will complete these steps by July 31, 2013. The actions that DHS has planned or under way should help address the intent of the recommendations. DHS also provided technical comments, which we incorporated as appropriate.

As agreed with your offices, unless you publicly announce its contents earlier, we plan no further distribution of this report until 30 days after its issue date. If you or your staff have any questions about this report, please contact me at (202) 512-8777 or gamblerr@gao.gov. Contact points for our Offices of Congressional Relations and Public Affairs may be found on the last page of this report. Key contributors to this report are listed in appendix III.

Rebecca Gambler
Acting Director
Homeland Security and Justice

Appendix I: Scope and Methodology

To examine data on arrests of and allegations against U.S. Customs and Border Protection (CBP) employees accused of corruption or misconduct issues, we analyzed data on 144 CBP employees arrested or indicted from fiscal year 2005 through fiscal year 2012 for corruption activities. We also analyzed data on allegations of corruption and misconduct against CBP employees from fiscal years 2006 through 2011. For both arrest and allegation data, these are the time periods for which the most complete data were available. In particular, we analyzed variations in both sets of data across CBP components and geographic region. To assess the reliability of these data, we (1) performed electronic data testing and looked for obvious errors in accuracy and completeness, and (2) interviewed agency officials knowledgeable about these data to determine the processes in place to ensure their accuracy. We determined that the data were sufficiently reliable for the purposes of this report. In addition, we interviewed officials from CBP Office of Internal Affairs (IA), Office of Field Operations (OFO), United States Border Patrol (USBP), and CBP's Human Resource Management, and Labor and Employee Relations, to gain their perspectives on these data on CBP employee corruption and misconduct.

To evaluate CBP's implementation of integrity-related controls to prevent and detect employee misconduct and corruption, we analyzed relevant laws such as the Anti-Corruption Border Act of 2010, which requires, by January 2013, that all CBP officer (CBPO) and U.S. Border Patrol Agent (BPA) applicants receive polygraph examinations before they are hired.[1] We also reviewed documentation on CBP's preemployment screening practices and their results—including background investigations and polygraph examinations—and relevant data and documentation on the random drug testing program and the periodic reinvestigation process for incumbent CBPOs and BPAs. In particular, we evaluated CBP IA data on the technical results of polygraph examinations from January 2008 through August 2012. To assess the reliability of the technical results of the polygraph data, we (1) performed electronic data testing and looked for obvious errors in accuracy and completeness, and (2) interviewed agency officials knowledgeable about these data to determine the processes in place to ensure their accuracy. We determined that these data were sufficiently reliable for the purposes of this report. In addition, we examined CBP IA's quality assurance program for its Personnel

---

[1]Pub. L. No. 111-376, § 3, 124 Stat. 4104, 4104-05 (2011).

Security Division (PSD),[2] including interviewing PSD officials who are responsible for deciding whether an applicant or incumbent officer or agent is suitable for hire or continued employment.[3] We also analyzed Human Resource Management's random drug testing data for fiscal years 2009 through 2011, the time period for which the most complete data were available, and examined the results of those mandated periodic reinvestigations that CBP IA had completed as of September 2012. To assess the reliability of these data, we conducted tests for accuracy and interviewed officials responsible for managing the drug testing and reinvestigation programs and found that the data were sufficiently reliable for the purposes of our report.

We compared CBP's integrity-related controls, as applicable, against recommended controls in *Standards for Internal Control in the Federal Government*[4] and standard practices from the Project Management Institute.[5] Furthermore, we conducted site visits to four locations along the southwest U.S. border to observe the implementation of various integrity-related controls and obtain perspectives from CBP IA, OFO, and USBP officials at these locations on the implementation of integrity-related controls. We conducted these visits in El Paso, Texas; Laredo, Texas; San Diego, California; and, Tucson, Arizona. We selected these locations on the basis of a variety of factors, including the colocation of CBP IA with OFO offices and USBP sectors along the southwest border and the number of allegations against or arrests of CBP employees for corruption or misconduct. Because we selected a nonprobability sample of sites, the information we obtained from these interviews and visits cannot be generalized to all OFO, USBP, and CBP IA field locations.

---

[2]PSD, within CBP IA, manages the personnel security and suitability program by initiating and adjudicating preemployment investigations for CBP applicants and contractors. PSD also conducts and adjudicates periodic reinvestigations and issues security clearances for CBP employees.

[3]With a favorable suitability determination, an applicant can be hired, if all other requirements are met. The suitability determination is a process that subjects applicants' and employees' personal conduct to evaluation throughout their careers. Title 5, Code of Federal Regulations Part 731, establishes factors that are used to make a determination of suitability.

[4]GAO, *Standards for Internal Control in the Federal Government*, GAO/AIMD-00-21.3.1 (Washington, D.C.: Nov. 1, 1999).

[5]Project Management Institute, *The Standard for Program Management*, second edition © (Newton Square, Pa., 2006, updated 2008).

However, observations obtained from these visits provided us with a greater understanding of CBP's integrity-related initiatives.

To evaluate CBP's integrity strategy, including how the agency incorporates lessons learned from prior misconduct and corruption cases, we reviewed documentation on integrity initiatives from CBP IA, OFO, and USBP, as well as from the Integrity Integrated Planning and Coordination Committee (IPCC), which CBP convened in 2011 as a forum to discuss integrity-related issues and ideas and to share standard practices among the members. In particular, we analyzed these documents against the requirements set forth in the CBP *Fiscal Year 2009-2014 Strategic Plan*.[6] In addition, we analyzed all available postcorruption analyses reports, which identify deficiencies that may have enabled CBP employees to engage in corruption-related activities, against OFO and USBP program requirements. We interviewed officials in Washington, D.C., from the Office of Policy and Planning, CBP IA, USBP, OFO, and IPCC, as well as officials during our site visits, regarding CBP's integrity strategy and the extent to which CBP is using lessons learned from prior corruption and misconduct cases to guide changes in policies and procedures, as appropriate.[7]

We conducted this performance audit from December 2011 to December 2012, in accordance with generally accepted government auditing standards. Those standards require that we plan and perform the audit to obtain sufficient, appropriate evidence to provide a reasonable basis for our findings and conclusions based on our audit objectives. We believe that the evidence obtained provides a reasonable basis for our findings and conclusions based on our audit objectives.

---

[6]U.S. Customs and Border Protection. *Secure Borders, Safe Travel, Legal Trade: U.S. Customs and Border Protection Fiscal Year 2009-2014 Strategic* Plan. Washington, D.C.: July 2009.

[7]CBP's Office of Policy and Planning is headed by an Executive Director and provides oversight of CBP policy and aligns policies across the various CBP components.

Appendix II: Comments from the Department of Homeland Security

U.S. Department of Homeland Security
Washington, DC 20528

November 27, 2012

Rebecca Gambler
Acting Director, Homeland Security and Justice Issues
U.S. Government Accountability Office
441 G Street, NW
Washington, DC 20548

Re: Draft Report GAO-13-59, "BORDER SECURITY: Additional Actions Needed to
Strengthen CBP Efforts to Mitigate Risk of Employee Corruption and Misconduct"

Dear Ms. Gambler:

Thank you for the opportunity to review and comment on this draft report. The U.S. Department
of Homeland Security (DHS) appreciates the U.S. Government Accountability Office's (GAO's)
work in planning and conducting its review and issuing this report.

DHS is pleased that GAO recognizes U.S. Customs and Border Protection's (CBP's) efforts to
deter corruption and ensure the integrity of its workforce. Any act of employee corruption
interferes with the Agency's mission to secure the Nation's borders against all threats and
facilitate legitimate travel and trade. We appreciate the acknowledgement that CBP is
proactively working to address the negative impact of mission-compromising corruption on
Agency-wide integrity.

As the draft report acknowledges, CBP conducts various integrity programs, such as background
investigations, periodic reinvestigations, and polygraphs, which are vital to CBP's goal of
employing and retaining employees of the highest caliber. For Fiscal Year (FY) 2012, CBP
opened roughly 15,000 background investigations for applicants, more than 10,000 periodic
reinvestigations for employees, and performed almost 5,000 polygraph exams. The draft report
appropriately underscores the critical value of these programs and identifies opportunity for
strengthening their effectiveness.

CBP's research and analysis programs give CBP crucial insight, which may be leveraged when
making decisions on the suitability of candidates for employment or detection of misconduct by
on-board employees and aids in deterring potential corruption among its existing employees.
The CBP Office of Internal Affairs (IA) Integrity Programs Division (IPD) is studying whether
there are any common traits found in the background investigations of employees who engage in
corruption or misconduct and the effect of an employee being stationed for duty in their

hometown. This research is also used for developing and administering integrity-related
training.

GAO's recommendations include having CBP IA undertake additional duties and responsibilities
not currently performed, such as periodically polygraphing incumbent law enforcement officers.
While DHS agrees these operations can be strengthened, we note these additional duties could
adversely impact Personnel Security Division (PSD) and Credibility Assessment Division (CAD)
resources if the new requirements are implemented without additional resources to accomplish
them. Between August 2006 and December 2008, mandated hiring surges doubled the size of
the Border Patrol (BP) from roughly 10,000 Border Patrol Agents (BPAs) to just over 20,000
BPAs, but additional resources were not dedicated to CBP IA's PSD and CAD. As a result,
CAD polygraph and PSD intake and adjudicative resources were significantly impacted. An
additional hiring surge of 1,000 BPAs and 350 CBP officers during the second half of
FY 2011 also resulted in further strain.

The draft report contained seven recommendations with which the Department concurs.
Specifically, GAO recommended that the CBP Commissioner:

Recommendation 1: Develop a mechanism to maintain and track data on the sources of
information (e.g., background investigation or polygraph examinations) that PSD uses to
determine what applicants are not suitable for hire to help CBP IA assess the effectiveness of its
applicant screening tools.

Response: Concur. CBP IA will collect data relative to the impact of the polygraph
examination on the outcome of CBP applicant suitability adjudications. To ensure the reliability
of the polygraph data collected, CBP is creating a "bridge" between the DHS Integrated Security
Management System (ISMS), which is PSD's official system of record and prescribed system for
all DHS Component use, and the IA Security Management Assessment Risk Tool, an integrated
database and workflow management tool being employed by CAD. This undertaking will
transmit CAD-related data to ISMS, thereby ensuring congruency between the related data in the
systems. Estimated Completion Date (ECD): March 31, 2013

Recommendation 2: Assess the feasibility of expanding the polygraph program to incumbent
CBPOs and BPAs, including the associated costs and benefits, options for how the agency will
use the results of the examinations, and the trade-offs associated with testing incumbent officers
and agents at various frequencies.

Response: Concur. CBP IA will work with the DHS Office of the Secretary, the DHS Office of
Chief Human Capital Officer, the DHS Office of the Chief Security Officer, and the U.S. Office
of Personnel Management (OPM) to explore the feasibility of expanding the polygraph program
to incumbent law enforcement officers, including Customs and Border Protection Officers
(CBPOs) and BPAs. CBP anticipates resistance to this proposal from the unions representing
our employees who are collective bargaining unit members. Initiating a polygraph exam for
incumbent employees may be viewed as a change to the conditions of employment, and the
unions may resist this change. CBP Labor Relations and the Office of Chief Counsel are
exploring these issues, and will be part of ongoing meetings to move this proposal forward.

2

Authorization from OPM is also required to conduct polygraph examinations of employees who are in competitive service appointments with CBP. OPM requires that a proposal to test any competitive service employees be endorsed at the department level, and that the CBP polygraph program adhere to federal standards for polygraph examinations. These standards include a biennial inspection of the CBP polygraph program by the National Center for Credibility Assessment, Quality Assurance Program, which reviews the administrative and field operations of the program for compliance with 118 federally established criteria. CBP complies with all of these requirements and a final report detailing those operations was sent to OPM on March 18, 2011, and a successful rating of the program is required as a condition for the renewal of polygraph authority. If the concept is approved, CBP will create an implementation plan with milestones identified. ECD: September 30, 2013

Recommendation 3: Conduct quality assurance reviews of CBP IA's adjudications of background investigations and periodic re-investigations, as required by PSD's quality assurance program.

Response: Concur. CBP IA-PSD will work to strengthen current Quality Assurance processes to verify the accuracy of the data collected, which will reinforce CBP's overall efforts to ensure reliability. Strengthening measures will include applying the expertise of current PSD staff to perform Quality Assurance reviews, providing objective feedback regarding the suitability/security review process and efficiencies, review of final adjudicative products, and implementation of best practices. The process will also entail reviewing cases to ensure compliance with applicable Executive Orders, Regulations, and DHS and CBP policies and procedures. ECD: February 28, 2013

Recommendation 4: Establish a process to fully document, as required, any deficiencies identified through PSD's quality assurance reviews.

Response: Concur. CBP IA-PSD will develop a process to document all deficiencies identified during Quality Assurance reviews. Reviewers will be required to complete a Quality Assurance Worksheet for each case to document the results. PSD will then develop a summary of any noted deficiencies for additional corrective action as deemed appropriate. CBP will determine whether there is a need for additional training or revised written guidance and/or operating procedures to address the documented deficiencies. ECD: February 28, 2013

Recommendation 5: Develop detailed guidance within OFO on the roles and responsibilities for integrity officers, in consultation with the appropriate stakeholders, such as CBP IA.

Response: Concur. CBP's Office of Field Operations' (OFO's) Incident Management Office will meet with the OFO Integrity Committee — composed of representatives from CBP IA, Office of Border Patrol (OBP), Labor and Employee Relations, and OFO - to develop detailed guidance on duties, roles, and responsibilities for Integrity Officers. ECD: June 30, 2013

Recommendation 6: Set target timelines for completing and implementing a comprehensive integrity strategy.

3

Response: Concur. CBP's Office of Policy and Planning (OPP) has prepared an initial plan of action and milestones for developing the recommended strategy, and efforts to implement it are currently underway. CBP OPP intends to use, in part, the existing CBP IA Integrity Strategy as a baseline for the CBP Comprehensive Integrity Strategy. CBP IA circulated the existing Integrity Strategy to the Integrity Integrated Planning and Coordination Cell (IPCC) for review and comment in September 2012.

The Integrity IPCC plans to convene in late 2012 to review comments on the IA Integrity Strategy and will develop an initial blueprint for the new comprehensive strategic document on the basis of the outcomes of this meeting. Additionally, CBP OPP and CBP IA will collaborate to determine ways both GAO's and the Homeland Security Institute's recommendations will contribute to defining a more clear direction for Integrity IPCC goals and objectives. These collective efforts will dictate the primary direction of the CBP Comprehensive Integrity Strategy, which CBP OPP believes will be completed within 4 months of identifying agency mission priorities. ECD: March 31, 2013

Recommendation 7: Complete OFO and BP post-corruption analysis reports for all CBPOs and BPAs who have been convicted of corruption-related activities, to the extent that information is available.

Response: Concur. CBP OFO and OBP will develop post-corruption analysis (PCA) reports for any convictions that do not currently have PCA reports. OBP and OFO understand the importance of these reports and value the information that can be derived from them. For cases which the necessary information to complete a full PCA report is not available, we will prepare modified reports, as appropriate. ECD: July 31, 2013

Again, thank you for the opportunity to review and comment on this draft report. Technical comments were previously provided under separate cover. Please feel free to contact me if you have any questions. We look forward to working with you in the future.

Sincerely,

Jim H. Crumpacker
Director
Departmental GAO-OIG Liaison Office

4

Appendix III: GAO Contact and Staff Acknowledgments

GAO Contact	Rebecca Gambler, (202) 512-8777 or gamblerr@gao.gov
Staff Acknowledgments	In addition to the contact named above, Kathryn Bernet, Assistant Director; David Alexander; Nanette J. Barton; Frances Cook; Wendy Dye; David Greyer; Jackson Hufnagle; Wendy Johnson; Otis S. Martin; and Linda Miller made significant contributions to the work.